THE CIVIL WAR

An Illustrated Guide

JG PRESS

Published by World Publications Group, Inc.
140 Laurel Street
East Bridgewater, MA 02333
www.wrldpub.com

Credits
Thanks to Ray Bonds who contributed to much of the
text. All photographs and other illustrations are from the
Library of Congress, Print and Photograph collection.
The color images on pages 2, 6, and 27 are from the
Carol M. Highsmith collection at the Library of
Congress.

Copyright © 2014 Greene Media Ltd

ISBN 978-1-4643-0399-9

A note on figures: Unless specified, casualty figures are estimates and include killed, wounded, and missing. Where specific figures are given, they should be treated with caution: records have been found to have been faulty and are the subject of much debate. A recent example of such debate is Binghamton University professor Dr. J. David Hacker's study of census information that suggests the traditional figure of 620,000, put forward by Union veterans William F. Fox and Thomas Leonard Livermore in 1889 after an exhaustive study of the army documents and pension records available at the time, could be understated by as many as 200,000 lives. One thing to remember is that disease was the main killer of the war: for every three soldiers killed in combat five died from disease.

PAGE 1: Kurz & Allison lithograph of the battle of Nashville.

LEFT: The battlefield of Bull Run is preserved as the Manassas National Battlefield Park by the National Park Service.

Contents

ABOVE: There are many memorials on the Civil War battlefields. This one remembers the 1st Ohio Infantry on the Chickamauga National Battlefield. Over two million Federal and a million Confederate men fought in the war. Some 220,000 combatants died in action: the figure increases to 625,000 including all deaths—from disease, accidents, wounds etc.

Introduction

War Between the States

Fought between the northern Union and the southern Confederacy, the Civil War had many causes but much of the argument revolved around who had preeminence—the individual state or the greater Union. Whatever the background, it pitched the smaller, agricultural, slave-owning Confederacy against the larger, more industrialized North.

On paper at least, the war should have been short-lived. The North, which was most likely to triumph in a prolonged conflict, had the greater resources in virtually every sense, yet the bloody conflict was to last from April 1861, when Union-held Fort Sumter was bombarded by Southern artillery, to May 1865, when the last Southern troops in the field laid down their arms. However, the South did have some advantages in the first years of the war—its troops tended to perform better, its commanders were the more able, and many battles were fought on home (Southern) terrain. The war was fought largely by citizen-soldiers, since the peacetime U.S. Army was tiny and the new soldiers had to adapt their fighting modes to reflect various advances in military technology that vastly increased the range and lethality of weapons.

The war began with rigid linear formations and even cavalry charges, but would gradually evolve into one in which more flexible battlefield formations, the use of natural cover, and siege warfare would become increasingly prevalent. Nevertheless, the war remains the most sanguine in United States history. The bloodiest single-day battle came early—on December 17, 1862—when almost 23,000 Union and Confederate troops became casualties (killed and wounded) during the battle of Antietam.

The land war was largely fought in two main theaters, effectively the area between the rival capitals, Washington and Richmond, which lay a mere 100 miles or so apart, and along the Mississippi River. For the first years of the war in the former theater, both sides attempted to capture the other's capital but were largely frustrated, although in their invasions of the North the Confederates had the upper hand on the battlefield. It was not until 1863 that the war can be said to have swung decisively in favor of the Union—the battle of Gettysburg, fought over July 1–3, ended all hope of the South ever taking Washington. Equally significant, if less lauded, was the North's capture of Vicksburg on July 4, an event that split the South in two, giving the North control of the Mississippi, and putting pressure on the eastern Confederate's ability to supply armies in the field.

Pressure from the North steadily mounted as the war entered its final phase, especially when the Union's naval blockade of the South, the Anaconda Plan, really began to bite. The war became less and less one of maneuver and was increasingly about attrition—the North simply began to grind down the South's ability to wage war. The

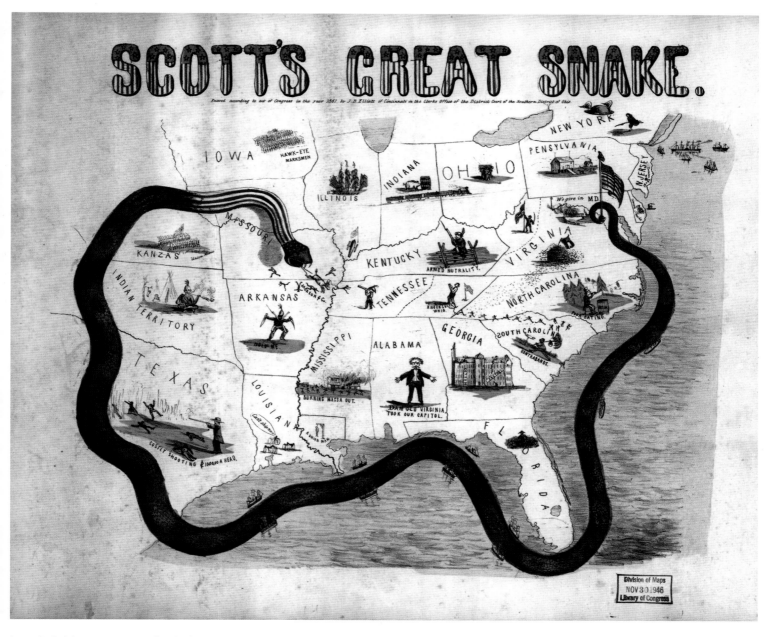

latter's field armies were slowly battered into submission in various bloody encounters, while its limited industrial base and agricultural heart were ravaged, not least by General Sherman's 300-mile "March to the Sea" from Atlanta to Savannah in late 1864. The South's most renowned force, the Army of Northern Virginia, capitulated on April 9, 1865, and that presaged the end.

ABOVE: Lt. Gen. Winfield Scott's Anaconda Plan is brilliantly explained in this cartoon. Derided in the press, the blockade of the South by the U.S. Navy played a significant part in the Union victory.

Date: April 12–14, 1861
Commanders: Union—Maj. Robert Anderson; Confederate—Brig. Gen. Pierre Gustave Toutant Beauregard
Troop strengths: Union—48 guns plus 127 men; Confederate—30 cannon and 18 mortars plus c.500 men
Casualties: Union—2 killed and 4 wounded; Confederate—4 wounded

The First Battle of Fort Sumter

The election on November 6, 1860, of President Abraham Lincoln, a Republican with anti-slavery sentiments, led seven Southern states to secede from the Union to form the Confederate States of America. South Carolina led the way on December 20, and the Confederacy's first and only president, Jefferson Davis, was elected on February 9, 1861. The outgoing U.S. president, James Buchanan, made little effort to prevent the seizure of U.S. military installations across the seceding states, but a pair of regular officers acting on their own initiative saved two especially important strongpoints. One was Fort Pickens in Florida's Pensacola Bay, while the other was Fort Sumter, a somewhat incomplete pentagonal brick edifice around three miles offshore in the harbor of Charleston, SC. The officer responsible for the latter coup was Kentucky-born Robert Anderson.

In January 1861 Buchanan had sent a boat, the *Star of the West*, loaded with food and ammunition to Sumter but it had been forced to withdraw when fired on from the South Carolina mainland. Thereafter the state's authorities announced that no supplies of any kind were to be allowed to reach Anderson. Lincoln officially took office on March 4 and vowed in his inaugural address to "hold, occupy, and possess" federal property in the Confederacy. Anderson was by this stage acutely short of supplies, so the newly incumbent president, who had no intention of abandoning the fort but equally did not want to initiate hostilities by taking military action, ordered that a supply boat be dispatched in early April.

The Confederacy's response came on the 7th after they had been formally informed of Lincoln's intention. Beauregard, the Confederate commander in Charleston and, coincidentally, Anderson's artillery instructor

at West Point, severed Sumter's communications with the mainland and began to marshal forces around the harbor. Three days later the Confederate secretary of war, Leroy Pope Walker, ordered Beauregard to demand the fort's evacuation or bombard it into submission. Anderson's response to the ultimatum delivered on the 11th was to state that he would evacuate in four days time unless he was attacked or received further orders from Washington.

At 03:20 on the 12th Anderson received a note that read, "We have the honor to notify you that [Beauregard] will open fire in one hour from this time." At 04:30 Capt. George James, commanding an artillery battery on James Island, fired the first shot of the war from a 10-inch mortar. Sumter's reply did not come until daylight, but then its

ABOVE: The Confederate flag flies over Fort Sumter, on April 15, following the surrender of Major Anderson and his Union troops.

OPPOSITE: Carol Highsmith's photograph of one of two 50,000-pound Rodman guns remaining as exhibits at Fort Sumter.

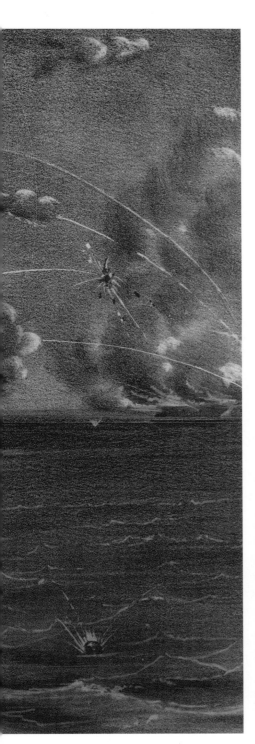

fire was intermittent due to a lack of artillerymen and ammunition. The appearance of a number of Union warships briefly gave the garrison hope, but they made no effort to intervene and soon sailed away.

The Confederate fire continued throughout the night and at dawn on the 13th other batteries, especially those at Fort Moultrie, added to the barrage. The fort's barracks were soon in flames and its cannon were reduced to firing just one shot every five minutes or so. A white flag was finally raised in the early afternoon and after some negotiating Anderson agreed to evacuate the next day.

Sumter had been hit by some 4,000 shells in thirty-four hours, yet neither side had suffered any deaths. That was soon to change as the garrison stood to attention to salute the Stars and Stripes before it was lowered. Sparks from a smoldering fire ignited a paper-wrapped cannon cartridge and the explosion produced six casualties one of whom, Private Daniel Hough, was the war's first fatality.

LEFT: The bombardment of Fort Sumter started on April 12, 1861.

BELOW: Postwar view of the defenses of Fort Sumter.

Date: July 21, 1861
Commanders: Union—Brig. Gen. Irvin McDowell; Confederate—Brig. Gen. Joseph Eggleston Johnston
Troop strengths: Union—c.38,000; Confederate—c. 35,500
Casualties: Union—2,896 (460 killed, 1,124 wounded, and 1,312 missing); Confederate—1,982 (387 killed, 1,582 wounded, and 13 missing)

The First Battle of Bull Run

The Confederacy's leadership knew that its best chance of securing independence was to strike fast and hard against the Union capital, Washington, with its main field force under Beauregard. Equally, the federal authorities believed that the war would be won if they captured the South's capital, Richmond. By July 1861 Beauregard's 20,000 men were located in the vicinity of Manassas, VA, protecting a rail line into the Shenandoah Valley, where a second Confederate army, 12,000 troops under Brig. Gen. Joseph E. Johnston, was facing some 18,000 Union troops under Maj. Gen. Robert Preston. Johnston was ordered to link up with Beauregard, who was positioned along Bull Run Creek, on the 18th, moving his entire command by train in what was a military first. It took just two days to move the bulk of the army some sixty miles. Union Brig. Gen. Irvin McDowell remained unaware that the transfer had taken place.

McDowell was under acute pressure to march on Richmond but would first have to deal with Beauregard. Bull Run was only really crossable at a small number of fords and one small bridge, so McDowell's options were limited. He decided to move from Centreville and launch a major strike against his opponent's left flank in a maneuver to isolate Beauregard from Johnston. The attack got underway on the morning of the 21st, but McDowell's opening gambit, a feint attack directed towards Mitchell's Ford Bridge, was spotted for what it really was. His main force crossed over Bull Run at the Stone Bridge and Sudley Springs Ford and then bore down on the Confederate left. The use of signal flags, another battlefield first, alerted Beauregard to the danger and, just in time, he was able to funnel reinforcements to his exposed left, particularly the area around Henry Hill.

There the battle raged at its most intense and it was there that one Confederate brigade commander, Brig. Gen. Thomas Jackson, kept his nerve during the bitter two-hour battle for

Henry Hill, earning himself the nickname "Stonewall." The battle turned at around 16:00, thanks to the arrival of two fresh Confederate brigades, one of them the last of Johnston's units to reach the battlefield by train. These proceeded to roll up McDowell's right flank. As they retreated under these unexpected hammer blows, some Union units began to panic and simply fled all the way back to Washington. For their part, the Confederates were too exhausted and disorganized to pursue their opponents. The battle fizzled out.

Bull Run was the largest engagement so far fought in North America but it was largely inconclusive, although the South could claim a victory. Washington did not fall, however, and the war would go on. Nevertheless, defeat came as a profound shock to the North, while the narrow victory reinforced the common view among the Confederates that they were martially superior to their opponents. In reality, the performance of the troops on both sides, the vast majority of whom were non-professional, was decidedly mixed.

ABOVE: Brig. Gen. Irvin McDowell (center, with goatee) and his staff at Arlington before his first offensive. Capt. James B. Fry, his adjutant, stands to McDowell's right, arms folded. McDowell (1818–85) is remembered for his defeat at the first Bull Run and his contribution to the Union defeat in the second.

LEFT: Judge Abram B. Olin of the District of Columbia Supreme Court (standing by the rail) delivered the address at the dedication of the battle monument at Bull Run, June 10, 1865.

ABOVE: The old stone house in the center of the Manassas Civil War battlefield site near Bull Run.

LEFT: "The daring charge" on the batteries at Bull Run by three companies of the 1st Regiment, Massachusetts Volunteer Infantry, commanded by Lt. Col. George Duncan Wells.

BELOW: Alfred Waud's sketch of Ambrose Burnside (on horseback with the profuse facial hair that led to the word "sideburns" entering the language) and his brigade during the battle. (See page 25 for information on this wonderful artist.)

Date: February 6–16, 1862
Commanders: Union—Brig. Gen.
Ulysses S. Grant; Flag Officer
Andrew H. Foote (Union Navy);
Confederate—Brig. Gen. Lloyd
Tilghman (Fort Henry), Brig. Gen.
Simon B. Buckner (Fort Donelson)
Troop strengths: Union—15,000;
Confederate—3,000+ (Fort Henry),
11,500+ (Fort Donelson)
Casualties: Union—40;
Confederate—79 (Fort Henry);
Union—2,331; Confederate—15,067
(Fort Donelson)

Taking Forts Henry and Donelson

The proximity of the Union and Confederate capitals in the east meant that much of the initial focus of the war was in Virginia. However, in 1862 the war exploded to the west of the Appalachians, along the Mississippi in Tennessee and later in Kentucky. The Mississippi was a key component of General-in-Chief Winfield Scott's strategic plan—nicknamed the Anaconda Plan (see pages 4–5)—that involved a naval blockade of the south with a thrust down the Mississippi to cut the Confederacy in two. The first step was the capture of the two forts, Henry on the Tennessee River and Donelson on the Cumberland.

Under the command of Brig. Gen. Ulysses S. Grant, two divisions landed north of Fort Henry on February 4–5, 1862. But by the time they reached the fort, its garrison had withdrawn and the fort, inundated by river flooding and bombarded by Union Navy gunboats, had surrendered.

Grant headed after the garrison, who retreated to the east of Fort Donelson, whose troops, under Brig. Gen. John B. Floyd, tried to break out of Grant's siege lines. They failed and, trapped in the fort, Brig. Gen. Simon B. Buckner had little option but to surrender.

RIGHT: Currier & Ives' depiction of the bombardment of Fort Henry by Foote's seven gunboats. It started on February 6. Return fire by the fort led to severe damage of *Essex* which killed and wounded 32 men including her commander, William D. Porter.

These victories were significant for a number of reasons. To begin with, they were the first major victories for the Union in the war; they also ensured Kentucky stayed in the Union, opened up the Tennessee River into Alabama (as was shown effectively with a raid along the river between February 6 and February 12). Finally, they brought attention to Grant, who was promoted major-general, gained the nickname "Unconditional Surrender" Grant, and set himself on a path that would lead him to all-over command of the Union armies and, thereafter, the presidency.

ABOVE: Andrew Hull Foote (1806–63) received the Thanks of Congress after the successful capture of forts Henry and Donelson and was made rear admiral in 1862. He died in 1863 while en route to take command of the South Atlantic Blockading Squadron.

ABOVE: Fort Donelson and the surrounding area, including the Cumberland River, the town of Dover, and Fort Henry Road, and the locations of Confederate earthworks as well as roads, buildings, woods, and creeks. It was drawn up by Robert Knox Sneden (1832–1918), a painter, mapmaker, and draftsman who was imprisoned in the notorious Andersonville Prison but still produced a huge collection of works.

RIGHT: Brig. Gen. Simon B. Buckner (1823–1914) surrendered Fort Donelson to Grant. He was the first Confederate general to surrender an army, and after entering captivity was exchanged in August 1862 for Brig. Gen. George A. McCall. Buckner ended the war as a lieutenant-general and commander of the Department of East Tennessee. A system for prisoner exchange was agreed by Generals John Dix (Union) and D. H. Hill (Confederate) in July 1862. The rate of exchange was set at one general for every 60 enlisted men, a colonel for 15, a lieutenant for 4, and a sergeant for 2. Grant stopped these exchanges in March 1864 because he said that they favored the Confederacy.

Date: April 6–7, 1862
Commanders: Union—Maj. Gen. Ulysses S. Grant; Confederate—Gen. Albert S. Johnston, Brig. Gen. Pierre Gustave Toutant Beauregard
Troop strengths: Union—62,700; Confederate—40,000
Casualties: Union—13,000 (1,754 killed, 8,408 wounded, and 2,885 missing); Confederate—10,500 (1,723 killed, 8,012 wounded, and 959 missing)

The Battle of Shiloh

The Confederate cause in Tennessee had suffered a number of reverses in February 1862. As we have seen, Grant captured Fort Henry on the Tennessee River on the 6th and went on to secure the unconditional surrender of Fort Donelson on the Cumberland River on the 16th. The state capital, Nashville, fell to Maj. Gen. Don Carlos Buell in the last week of the same month. Johnston temporarily abandoned the state, moving some 40,000 men to Corinth just over the border with Mississippi. Grant followed with a similar number of troops but was ordered to halt on the banks of the Tennessee River around Pittsburg Landing and Shiloh Church, some twenty-two miles north of Corinth, and await the arrival of Buell's troops from Nashville.

OPPOSITE: "The Hornet's Nest" after Thure de Thulstrup's painting published in *Prang's War Pictures*. The epicenter of the battle, here on the left of the sunken road, is Hinckenlooper's battery. To the right the troops of Prentiss' division; beyond are those of W.H.L. Wallace. The painting was produced as a print by Louis Prang & Co and appeared in its set of chromolithographs, *Prang's War Pictures*. There were 18 prints in all: 6 of eastern battles, 6 of western battles, and 6 naval images. A number of them appear throughout this book.

LEFT: Gen. Albert Sidney Johnston (1803–62) died at Shiloh. It was his surprise attack on Grant that so nearly defeated the Union forces. Johnston was hit in the leg, probably by friendly fire, and died from loss of blood.

BELOW: Gen. Don Carlos Buell reinforced Grant for the second day of battle at Shiloh and his men contributed significantly to the Union success that day, although Buell himself, a rival of Grant's, was said to have been slow to commit his troops.

Beauregard, who was Johnston's second-in-command with the Army of the Mississippi, persuaded his superior to launch a surprise attack before Buell and Grant linked up. Johnston agreed, and the move north began on April 3. Rain, rough terrain, and logistical problems delayed the advance, so that the attack did not begin until the early morning of the 6th. The battle opened before daylight and the Confederates steamrollered a succession of forward Union positions. After three hours of fighting, Johnston's leading units had pushed the Union right flank back nearly a mile.

The Confederates now concentrated their efforts on the Union center, but at least a dozen attacks against a stoutly defended area—it became known as the Hornet's Nest —were thrown back. The fighting in the center also precluded the Confederates from launching their intended strike against Grant's left flank. Matters were made worse at 14:40 when Johnston died after having an artery in his leg severed by a stray bullet, probably fired from his own side. Beauregard took his place. The only good news came at around three hours later when Beauregard heard that the Hornet's Nest was finally taken, but the fighting then ebbed away with sunset.

The Confederates had received intelligence that Buell was near Decatur, northern Alabama, but, in fact, his troops had begun crossing the Tennessee River during the late afternoon of the first day of the battle. One of Grant's own divisions had also arrived at Shiloh and, with these reinforcements more than making up for his losses, he went over to the attack on the 7th. Beauregard, who had no reinforcements to call on, ordered his troops to stand fast, and for much of the day they held off the Union forces. However, by the mid-afternoon it was clear to Beauregard that not only was he losing, but he also was risking wholesale defeat if he stayed at Shiloh. Accordingly, he ordered his army back to Corinth.

Both sides claim Shiloh as a victory, but Grant had the better case. He retained possession of the battlefield, the greater part of Tennessee remained under Union control, and he and Buell had successfully linked up. In late May the Confederates abandoned Corinth, and the greater part of western Tennessee, including Memphis, was thus lost to their cause.

RIGHT: The battle was bloody: around 3,500 died on the field of Shiloh.

Date: April 25–May 1, 1862
Commanders: Union—Flag Officer David G. Farragut and
Maj. Gen. Benjamin Franklin Butler;
Confederate—Maj. Gen. Mansfield Lovell
Troop strengths: Union—75,000;
Confederate—54,268
Casualties: Union—229;
Confederate—782; at New Orleans, none

ABOVE: David G. Farragut (1801–70) is revered as one of the greatest U.S. naval commanders. He was the first rear admiral, vice admiral, and admiral in the U.S. Navy.

The Capture of New Orleans

The strategic importance of New Orleans, at the mouth of the Mississippi, ensured that it was an early target for the Union—particularly so after Grant's successes further north.

The West Gulf Blockading Squadron was commanded by David G. Farragut, who had spent some of his early life in New Orleans, before joining the navy as a midshipman aged nine. After the death of his mother, in 1808 Farragut was adopted by naval officer David Porter. His adoptive brother, David Dixon Porter, commanded the flotilla of mortar boats during this campaign.

The keys to taking New Orleans were forts Jackson and St. Philip at the mouth of the river, the boom that lay between them, and the Chalmette artillery batteries. Defended by a ragtag collection of incomplete ironclads and gunboats, most of the Confederate defenses of New Orleans faced north, from where the main threat was adjudged to come.

Once Farragut's forces had negotiated the bar at the mouth of the Mississippi, Porter's mortars—21 schooners—were given a chance to bombard the forts into submission between April 18 and April 23. The 7,500 mortar rounds fired had a significant effect on the morale and fabric of the forts, but they did not reduce significantly the effectiveness of their batteries, forcing Farragut's vessels to run the gauntlet.

First, the boom had to be broken: this was achieved by gunboats *Kineo*, *Pinola*, and *Itasca*. On April 24 Farragut's squadron attacked. The disjointed battle

that followed, first as the forts' batteries engaged the Union vessels and then as the Confederate fleet attacked, ended in complete victory for the Union who lost only one ship. The Confederates lost twelve including the unfinished ironclads CSS *Louisiana*—which played a small part in the battle—and CSS *Mississippi*, which was destroyed by her captain rather than allowed to fall into Union hands.

The successful Union fleet passed the Chalmette batteries and threatened New Orleans, whose defending forces, under Gen. Mansfield Lovell, retreated, thus leaving the city—and the Mississippi toward Vicksburg—to the Union.

Back at the forts, Butler prepared an attack but it did not have a chance to start: the men in the forts, their morale broken by the bombardment and loss of New Orleans, mutinied and surrendered to David Dixon Porter. The last word was left to the captain of the *Louisiana*, moored near Fort St. Philip. He and his crew set their ship alight and she drifted away from the bank, exploding shortly after when flames reached her magazine.

ABOVE: Maj. Gen. Mansfield Lovell (1822–84) commanded New Orleans and was blamed for its loss to the Confederacy, later losing command of his infantry division. A court of inquiry in 1863 exonerated him of blame, but he did not receive another command.

LEFT: "Capture of New Orleans"—another of *Prang's War Pictures*, J.O. Davidson's painting shows Farragut's Mississippi squadron passing Forts Philip and Jackson in the early morning of April 24, 1862.

Date: March–July, 1862
Commanders: Union—Maj. Gen. George B. McClellan; Confederate—Gen. Joseph E. Johnston then Gen. Robert E. Lee
Troop strengths: Union—100,000; Confederate—43,000 increasing to 92,000 by the Seven Days' Battles
Casualties: Williamsburg: Union—2,283; Confederate—1,682. Fair Oaks/Seven Pines: Union—5,031 (790 killed, 3,594 wounded, 647 captured or missing); Confederate—6,134 (980 killed, 4,749 wounded, 405 captured or missing).
Seven Days' Battles: Union—15,800 (1,734 killed, 8,066 wounded, 6,055 missing/captured); Confederate—20,600 (3,494 killed, 15,758 wounded, 952 missing/captured)

The Peninsular Campaign

It was a brave idea: a huge seaborne assault on the Virginia Peninsula that would take the Confederates by surprise, allowing George B. McClellan's Army of the Potomac to take Richmond and end the war at a stroke. The first part of it, moving over 120,000 troops and all their supplies to land at Fort Monroe, was accomplished adroitly thanks to a fleet of 113 steamships, 188 schooners, and 88 barges—and the fact that the dangerous Confederate ironclad *Virginia* had been nullified by the Union ironclad *Monitor* at the battle of Hampton Roads on March 9.

Soon after landing, on April 4 the Union forces moved off, but a clever, deceptive defense by Gen. John Magruder led McClellan to slow his offensive, holding him up for a month on the Warwick Line, during which McClellan dug in to besiege Yorktown allowing the Confederates time to reinforce Magruder and shore up the defense of Richmond. Gen. Joseph E. Johnston took control of Confederate forces, and just before McClellan attacked, Johnston retreated on May 3.

RIGHT: McClellan's lines in front of Yorktown included many heavy guns whose size and weight speaks for the logistics involved in moving them. This is Battery No. 4 in May 1862. It had ten 13-inch mortars manned by the First Connecticut and Second New York Artillery.

The Union caught up with the Confederate army at Williamsburg. After an inconclusive battle, Johnston retreated again. In another bold move, McClellan sent Franklin's division up the York River to cut off Johnston's retreat, but Franklin was held at Eltham's Landing on May 7 by Brig. Gen. John Bell Hood's Texas Brigade and Johnston escaped.

At the other end of the peninsula, Abraham Lincoln was taking a personal hand in affairs. Arriving at Fort Monroe on May 6, he ordered an attack on Norfolk. The naval yard surrendered on May 10, and *Virginia* was destroyed because it couldn't negotiate the shallower waters of the River James. With the river open to the Union and a huge army landed, Richmond was severely threatened, but an exploratory attack by vessels of the North Atlantic Blockading Squadron was held below the Confederate capital by the guns of Fort Darling on Drewery's Bluff.

Johnston reached Richmond and McClellan—believing he was outnumbered and waiting for reinforcement by Brig. Gen. Irvin McDowell's I Corps from the north—slowly established his army around the swampy Chickahominy River. This had the advantage of covering McDowell's likely route, but the disadvantage of poor quartering for his troops who suffered awfully from disease.

On May 31 Johnston did what McClellan had not expected: he attacked. The battle at Seven Pines or Fair Oaks Station (as the Union named it) ended inconclusively on June 1, but it effectively ended McClellan's offensive in front of the city. It also saw a decisive moment in the Civil War. Johnston was wounded and Robert E. Lee took over command of what would become the Army of Northern Virginia.

A month-long stalemate followed before, on June 25, McClellan advanced toward Richmond and initiated what would be called the Seven Days' Battles at Oak Grove.

As "Stonewall" Jackson's division neared Richmond following the Shenandoah Valley Campaign, which crucially had kept Union reinforcements from the peninsula, Lee took the offensive. He planned for Jackson to attack the Union forces to the north of the Chickahominy, but Maj. Gen. A.P. Hill attacked first at Mechanicsville/Beaver Dam. While the Confederates lost nearly 1,500 men, McClellan retreated rather than making the most of his victory. Lee pushed on, fighting all day at Gaines' Mill and finally breaking the Union lines. McClellan retreated again but Lee was unable to produce a hammer blow at the battle of Glendale on June 30, and McClellan took up a strong position at Malvern Hill. When Lee attacked on July 1, he sustained 5,300 casualties and made no ground, but McClellan continued to retreat allowing Lee to turn his attention to North Virginia and Maj. Gen. John Pope's army.

McClellan had shown himself to be insufficiently decisive to push through his opportunities, constantly overestimating his enemy's numbers; that, and the disease the Union forces had suffered around the Chickahominy, proved more decisive than the Confederate armies.

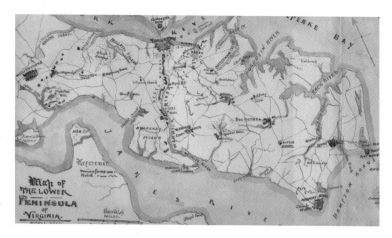

ABOVE: Sneden's map of the peninsula.

BELOW: Robert Edward Lee (1807–70) was the son of a Revolutionary War officer, a graduate of the U.S. Military Academy, and had spent 32 years in the U.S. Army. He was in charge of the troops who captured John Brown at Harpers Ferry and Winfield Scott had offered him overall command of Union forces, but when his state, Virginia, seceded, he resigned. After taking over from Johnston, Lee proved to be a brilliant tactician whose conduct and ability gained the respect of his enemies. After his surrender, he stood for reconciliation and reconstruction and when he died friend and foe alike mourned the passing of a great warrior.

Date: August 29–30, 1862
Commanders: Union—Maj. Gen.
John Pope; Confederate—Gen.
Robert E. Lee
Troop strengths: Union—75,000;
Confederate—54,268
Casualties: Union—16,000 (1,724
dead, 8,372 wounded and 5,958
missing); Confederate—9,000
(1,481 dead, 7,627 wounded and 89
missing)

The Second Battle of Bull Run

Pope had taken command of the Union's Army of Virginia on June 26, 1862, and over the next few weeks began to plan a campaign to capture the South's capital, Richmond. His 66,000 men were to be supplemented by elements of the Army of the Potomac, which had suffered a mauling outside the Southern capital during the Seven Days' Battles fought between June 25 and July 1. The Army of the Potomac received orders to move on August 3. If these two Union forces had been united they

would have a combined strength of more than 100,000 men. The main Confederate field force, Lee's Army of Northern Virginia, facing Pope along the Rappahannock River in central Virginia, comprised a mere 55,000 men.

When Lee received news of the Army of the Potomac's movement on August 24, he immediately realized that he had to strike first before the two Union armies could unite against him. That same day the Confederate commander ordered Maj. Gen. Thomas "Stonewall" Jackson's 12,000 men to march north and then east to get behind Pope's men in the vicinity of Manassas. Lee would follow with Lt. Gen. James Longstreet's corps. Jackson marched an epic fifty-four miles in high summer, reaching the vicinity of Manassas on the 27th. The next day he looted and burned Pope's supply dump at Manassas Junction and then took up a defensive position along the line of an incomplete railway cutting a little to the west of the First Bull Run battlefield of the previous year.

To further lure the Union commander into the trap, Jackson also deliberately revealed his precise location on the 28th by attacking a Union division at nearby Groveton. Pope reacted quickly and concentrated against Jackson the next day. Federal units launched several piecemeal and uncoordinated attacks against the Confederate line, but all were repulsed. Pope resolved to continue the fight the next day but, unbeknownst to him, Longstreet had nearly reached Jackson. The fighting on the 30th saw the Federal troops again assault Jackson's line. None of the attacks was successful, but Jackson's men were fast running out of ammunition and, indeed, some were forced to fling rocks at the Union troops.

Salvation came when Longstreet's command began its large-scale onslaught against the lightly defended and exposed left flank of Pope's force—exposed because the Union unit that would have defended against the attack, Fitz John Porter's V Corps, had been thrown in to the attack on Jackson. The Union line was rolled up and pushed back across Bull Run Creek. But, unlike the conclusion of the first battle, this time the withdrawal back to heavily defended Washington was conducted in generally good order. Lee ordered a follow-up the next day but called off the pursuit after Jackson was checked at the battle of Chantilly on September 1. Pope was relieved of command eleven days later and the Army of Virginia was absorbed into the Army of the Potomac.

ABOVE: Alfred Waud's study of the battle, showing the advance of Maj. Gen. Ambrose P. Hill's Light Division. Hill was on Jackson's left flank on Stony Ridge. Waud (1828–91) was an artist for the *New York Illustrated News* and then *Harper's Weekly*, and was at every battle of the Army of the Potomac from First Bull Run to the siege of Petersburg.

OPPOSITE: A Currier & Ives lithograph of the battle.

Date: September 17, 1862
Commanders: Union—Maj. Gen. George B. McClellan; Confederate—Gen. Robert E. Lee
Troop strengths: Union—80,000; Confederate—45,000
Casualties: Union—12,100 (2,108 killed and 10,032 wounded or missing); Confederate—13,700 (2,700 killed and 11,023 wounded or missing)

The Battle of Antietam

The first six months of 1862 had seen the Confederacy suffer a number of reverses in the various theaters of the war. Union forces had overrun around 50,000 square miles of its territory and the large Army of the Potomac under McClellan was advancing up the Virginia Peninsula to menace Richmond, capital of the South. Yet, within the space of a few months, the situation was utterly transformed, with the attack on the capital defeated and with Confederate troops within easy striking distance of Washington. The catalyst of change was Robert E. Lee, and the newly created Army of Northern Virginia.

After victory at the Second Battle of Bull Run in late August, Lee paused briefly and then launched an invasion of the North, with his troops beginning to cross the Potomac River on September 4. McClellan, only recently appointed to command of the Army of the Potomac, moved northward along the same river, looking for Lee. McClellan had the good fortune to discover a copy of Lee's invasion orders at Frederick, MD, on the 14th. These showed that, at that time, Lee's Army of Northern Virginia was divided into five parts to carry out various tasks. Yet McClellan continued to move

RIGHT: "Advance on the Rebel Center at Dunker Church." The battle of Antietam as portrayed by Thure de Thulstrup in *Prang's War Pictures.*

FAR RIGHT: Bloody Lane, Antietam, today. In 1862, there were some 5,600 casualties around the sunken lane, 3,000 from the Union and 2,600 Confederates.

lowly, thereby allowing Lee to largely reunite his scattered forces and ake up an excellent defensive position on high ground to the east of he town of Sharpsburg. His left flank rested on the Potomac, while his ront ran along Antietam Creek.

McClellan made the assumption that he was outnumbered (as he had done throughout the Peninsular Campaign) but finally attacked on the 17th. He planned to strike at Lee's left flank and then punch across the creek on the right. The early morning attack on the left flank was brought to a halt with heavy casualties, not least along a sunken road later nicknamed "Bloody Lane." The action switched to Lee's center and right during the mid-morning. Union troops made three desperate attempts to take a narrow bridge, not realizing that the creek was fordable. Finally carried, it took the local commander some two hours to reorganize his various units before they began to push towards Sharpsburg—the Confederate name for the battle.

Yet, even as they neared the town, they were hit on the left flank when Ambrose P. Hill's fresh Confederate division arrived from Harpers Ferry, its commander wearing his red battle shirt. The Union line collapsed and fled back across the creek, thus ending the bloodiest day in U.S. military history. Lee had won a great tactical victory but began withdrawing back across the Potomac two days later. As his invasion was therefore over, the Union could claim the greater strategic victory. Antietam's even greater political significance was revealed on the 22nd when Lincoln felt confident enough to announce his provisional Emancipation Proclamation to free the South's slaves.

ABOVE: Alexander Gardner's photograph of the dead of the Louisiana Regiment taken two days after the battle. They are possibly from the Louisiana Tigers brigades in "Stonewall" Jackson's corps. They performed heroically on the field but paid a terrible price: of 550 Louisiana Tigers who advanced under Harry T. Hays only forty or so were able to rally around the colors at Dunker Church half an hour later. Forty-five had been killed, 289 were wounded, and two were missing.

BELOW: Two weeks after the battle Lincoln visited Gen. McClellan and toured the battlefield. He was accompanied by his old friend Gen. McClernand (right) and Allan Pinkerton (left). McClellan was relieved of his command on November 5.

Date: December 31, 1862–January 3, 1863

Commanders: Union—Maj. Gen. William Rosecrans; Confederate—Gen. Braxton Bragg

Troop strengths: Union—44,000; Confederate—38,000

Casualties: Union—12,900 (1,677 killed, 7,543 wounded, 3,686 captured/missing); Confederate—11,700 (1,294 killed, 7,945 wounded, 2,500 captured/missing)

The Battle of Stones River

The campaigning across Tennessee and Kentucky in the latter part of 1862 had seen Bragg's reinforced Army of Tennessee score a minor but important victory at Richmond, KY, on August 30; one that led Union Maj. Gen. Don Carlos Buell's Army of the Ohio to retreat to the Ohio River, thereby abandoning much of the state. Union reinforcements were sent and advanced back into Kentucky. A drawn battle took place at Perryville on October 8 and, somewhat unnecessarily, Bragg opted to fall back into Tennessee and take up positions around Murfreesboro to protect the railway line that ran from Nashville to Georgia. The tardy Buell was dismissed some two weeks later and replaced by Rosecrans, who reoccupied Nashville at the end of the first week of November.

For the next several weeks, and much to the chagrin of their respective political masters, neither general seemed in a hurry to strike at their opponent. Rosecrans was finally prodded into action towards the end of December and advanced the thirty miles from his base to Murfreesboro. Both generals decided to attack and both chose to do so with troops on their respective left wings. Bragg moved first, at around dawn on the 31st, and his advance caught the troops on the Union right flank by surprise. It simply fell apart and retreated rapidly. Rosecrans' center was made of sterner stuff, especially the division led by Brig. Gen. Philip Sheridan. By nightfall the Union commander was able to patch together a new defensive position along the line of the Nashville Turnpike.

The night was bitterly cold and the men were exhausted. It was hardly surprising that the two armies merely held their ground, and no major combat took place on New

RIGHT: Sketched by A.E. Mathews, of the 31st Regiment, Ohio Volunteer Infantry, this print shows Union artillery firing at Confederate troops.

LEFT: Kurz & Allison lithograph of the battle.

Year's Day. There was a briefly flurry of action on January 2, when two divisions clashed on Bragg's extreme right wing. The initial Union advance across Stones River was halted by the arrival of a Confederate division, but it, too, was repulsed by concentrated fire from some sixty Union field guns as it, in turn, tried to cross the river.

Bragg was informed on the 3rd that Rosecrans was about to receive substantial reinforcements, and he decided to withdraw. The movement began that night but Rosecrans decided against a pursuit. He ordered his troops to dig extensive field fortifications around Murfreesboro, and Bragg did likewise at his new base. Stones River was a tactical and strategic victory for the Union at a time when they were few and far between. Despite the heavy casualties, it gave a boost to the wider public's morale in the North.

BELOW LEFT: From another Mathews sketch, this shows the charge of the first brigade, commanded by Col. M. B. Walker, on the Friday evening, January 2, "in which the rebels were repulsed with heavy loss."

BELOW RIGHT: This print, from a Mathews sketch, shows the charge of Gen. Negley's Division—Col. John F. Miller's Brigade and Col. F.H. Stanley's Brigade—across the river on Friday, January 2. This counterattack completed the devastating repulse of Confederate Brig. Gen. John C. Breckinridge's attack.

Date: May 1–6, 1863
Commanders: Union—Maj. Gen. Joseph Hooker; Confederate—Gen. Robert E. Lee
Troop strengths: Union—130,000; Confederate—60,000
Casualties: Union—17,000 ((1,606 killed, 9,672 wounded, 5,919 captured/missing); Confederate—13,000 (1,665 killed, 9,081 wounded, 2,018 captured/missing)

The Battle of Chancellorsville

Maj. Gen. Hooker ("Fighting Joe") took command of the Army of the Potomac in January 1863 and, as a commander with a supposed unquenchable thirst for action, decided to launch his men against Lee's Army of Northern Virginia in a complex spring offensive designed to turn Lee's left flank at Fredericksburg, VA. The advance began on April 29, when Hooker led some 90,000 men across the Rappahannock River and took them into an area of very dense forest with few roads, ominously known as the Wilderness. He left a further 40,000 men under Gen. John Sedgwick, positioned directly opposite Lee at Fredericksburg.

Lee's response was to leave some 10,000 men under Gen. Jubal Early to cover Sedgwick and make a staged withdrawal if the latter decided to attack, and then he ordered the remainder of his command to move against Hooker's main force. Lt. Gen. Thomas "Stonewall" Jackson was told to circle around Hooker's right flank outside Chancellorsville, by way of Wilderness Tavern, while Lee with some 17,000 troops would take a more direct route toward Hooker's center.

RIGHT: Kurz & Allison lithograph of the Battle of Chancellorsville showing "Stonewall" Jackson shot.

The first contact came on May 1 and, despite his superior numbers, Hooker quickly lost his nerve and went onto the defensive. Jackson began his fifteen-mile march at 08:00 the next day and launched a ferocious assault on Hooker's right flank, as planned, at a little before dusk. The Union troops were overwhelmed and the whole wing disintegrated. Jackson sensed that total victory might be in sight and went forward to assess the situation, but was fired on and mortally wounded by his own troops. His command went to Maj. Gen. J. E. B. Stuart.

The 3rd saw Sedgwick push Early out of Fredericksburg and then try to move on Chancellorsville. Lee correctly sensed that Hooker was so knocked off balance by the recent events that he would largely remain inactive, so led some 25,000 men to aid Early. Sedgwick came close to being cut off near Salem Church but just managed to cross back over the Rappahannock on the 4th. Hooker followed him the next day and completed the retreat on the 6th. Chancellorsville was, undoubtedly, Lee's masterpiece, one in which he comprehensively outmaneuvered his more timid opponents so as to offset his significantly lower number of troops.

Nevertheless, the battle had cost the Army of Northern Virginia dear and the Confederacy did not have bottomless reserves of manpower. Jackson, who died of his wounds on the 10th, was irreplaceable. Hooker proposed a second two-pronged attack on Lee in June but his chastened superiors feared a second Chancellorsville, and vetoed his plan. The general tendered his resignation and it was accepted on the 28th, just days before the crucial battle of Gettysburg.

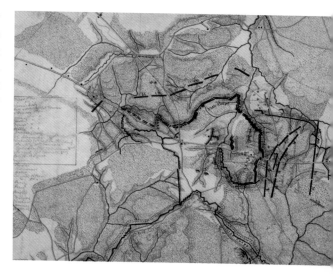

ABOVE: The positions of the forces on May 3.

LEFT: The place Jackson fell was commemorated and became a much-visited spot. He was a hero to the Confederacy and much esteemed by all. Shot by a Confederate picket, he died of complications from pneumonia eight days after his arm had been amputated. As he lay dying, Lee sent a message, "Give General Jackson my affectionate regards, and say to him: he has lost his left arm but I my right." Jackson's wife never remarried, and lived until 1915, known as the "Widow of the Confederacy." He is honored at the Virginia Military Institute—the West Point of the South—where a bronze statue of Jackson stands outside the main entrance to the cadet barracks. Jackson's unit, the Stonewall Brigade, still exists as the 116th Infantry Brigade of the U.S. Army, part of the Virginia National Guard. The shoulder sleeve insignia shows Stonewall Jackson mounted on horseback.

Vicksburg

Date: May 18–July 4, 1863
Commanders: Union—Maj. Gen. Ulysses S. Grant; Confederate—Gen. John C. Pemberton
Troop strengths: Union—77,000; Confederate—33,000
Casualties: Union—4,900 (c.800 killed, 3,940 wounded, 164 missing); Confederate—32,500 (c.800 killed, c.2,000 wounded, c.29,500 missing and surrendered)

Port Hudson

Date: May 22–July 9, 1863
Commanders: Union—Maj. Gen. Nathaniel P. Banks; Confederate—Gen. Franklin Gardner
Troop strengths: Union—30–40,000; Confederate—7,500
Casualties: Union—10,000 (including 5,000 to disease); Confederate—7,500 (1,000 dead and wounded, and 6,500 surrendered)

RIGHT: *Prang's War Pictures* included this Thure de Thulstrup painting of the siege of Vicksburg, showing the flag bearer of Union Gen. M. D. Leggett's Illinois nearing the top of Fort Hill.

Taking Vicksburg and Port Hudson

After taking New Orleans in spring 1862, Adm. David Farragut had sailed upriver to force Vicksburg to surrender. The lynchpin of Confederate communications between east and west, the city was well defended on a naturally imposing bluff dominating the river and would not be given up easily. Rebuffed, Farragut returned in June 1862, but in spite of shelling Vicksburg into July and attempting to bypass the city by digging a canal across the De Soto Peninsula, he got nowhere. By the time that the Union started to move toward Vicksburg in December, the city had been further reinforced. It had also been turned into a fortress comprising nine major forts connected by trenches, 172 big guns, and a garrison that neared 30,000.

The first stage in the campaign saw Grant advance down the Mississippi Railroad and Sherman down the river in a convoy commanded by Adm. David Porter. Sherman's attack petered out at the end of December at Chickasaw Bayou in the strongly defended Walnut Hills, northeast of Vicksburg. Grant, his supply lines harried by cavalry raids conducted by Maj. Gen. Earl van Dorn and Lt. Gen. Nathan Forrest, was also stymied.

The second stage saw the involvement of Lincoln who was convinced by Maj. Gen. John A. McClernand that a double attack—himself from the north and Maj. Gen. Nathaniel P. Banks from New Orleans—could win Vicksburg. McClernand was a politician rather than a military man, a friend and ally of Lincoln's, and had served under Grant in 1861–62. He arrived in Memphis in January and started his campaign by appropriating Sherman's forces and—at Sherman's suggestion but without telling Grant—by attacking Fort Hindman on the Arkansas River. The attack was successful, but unsurprisingly, Grant reacted strongly, relieving McClernand of command and incorporating his forces into his own. McClernand would agitate against Grant during the Vicksburg campaign until Grant dismissed him.

ABOVE: Kurz & Allison lithograph of the siege of Vicksburg.

Between January and March 1863 Grant made a number of attempts to close on Vicksburg by water, including returning to the earlier canal project, but none of them was successful.

Finally, in late March Grant decided on a strategy: he would march his troops down the western side of the river, cross south of the city, and then join forces with Maj. Gen. Nathaniel Banks to take Port Hudson before moving back to attack Vicksburg from the south and east. To this end, a 70-mile route was created from Milliken's Bend to New Carthage, where the Mississippi would be crossed. Next, Adm. Porter sent gunboats and stores downriver, passing under the guns of Vicksburg with only minor casualties in spite of the protracted, heavy bombardment from the Confederate batteries. Finally, Grant sent Sherman in a feint attack on Snyder's Bluff north of Vicksburg and Col. Benjamin Grierson on a raid through central Mississippi.

BELOW: Sneden's map shows the Union troops on land and water surrounding Confederate fortifications at Port Hudson on the Mississippi River, approximately 25 miles north of Baton Rouge. The Union XIX Corps under Gen. Banks had its first engagement on May 26 on the Bayou Sara Road, and laid siege to the fort on May 27. Confederate Gen. Franklin Gardner surrendered Port Hudson on July 9, 1863, after having been under siege for six weeks and upon hearing news of the fall of Vicksburg to Gen. Grant on July 4.

The feints—particularly Grierson's raid—drew troops away from the defense and Grant, after crossing the mighty river at Bruinsburg and holding onto his bridgehead at the battle of Port Gibson, decided to push on to Vicksburg rather than heading for Port Hudson. Reconnaissance showed him that the city's southern defenses were strong, so Grant marched east, defeating Joseph Johnston, taking Jackson, the Mississippi state capital, and severing Vicksburg's supply rail link. His forces then converged on Vicksburg driving the Confederates, who had advanced to join Johnston, before them, beating them at Champion Hill and Big Black Bridge, and finally investing the city on May 18. His army had marched more than 200 miles in seventeen days and brooked no opposition. Six weeks later, after having withstood major assaults on May 19 and 22, and June 25, under continuous bombardment, having no supplies, all attempts by Confederate forces outside to relieve the siege having failed, Lt. Gen. John C. Pemberton was forced to surrender on July 4.

A few days later, on July 9, Port Hudson fell. Besieged by Banks from May 27, the garrison put up a spirited resistance, repulsing a number of attacks, before surrendering after hearing that Vicksburg had fallen.

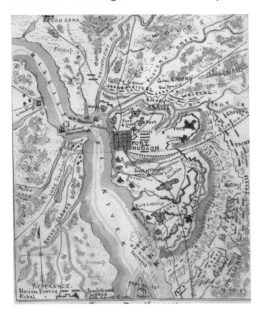

Date: July 1–3, 1863
Commanders: Union—Maj. Gen. George Meade; Confederate—Gen. Robert E. Lee
Troop strengths: Union—88,000; Confederate—75,000
Casualties: Union—23,000 (3,115 killed, 14,529 wounded, and 5,365 missing); Confederate—28,000 (2,500+ killed, c.13,000 wounded, and 5,425 missing)

The Battle of Gettysburg

The Battle of Chancellorsville in May 1863 had given Lee the strategic initiative and he determined to launch yet another invasion of the North. His Army of Northern Virginia crossed the Potomac River into the North between June 15 and 24. The commander of the Union's Army of the Potomac, Maj. Gen. Joseph Hooker, began to move his forces north to intercept Lee but missed repeated opportunities to hit the Confederate leader while his various corps were strung out on the line of march. When Hooker's plan of attack was opposed, he resigned on the 28th to be replaced by Meade—the army's fifth commander in just ten months.

RIGHT: Prang's "Gettysburg" by Thure de Thulstrup shows Gen. Alexander S. Webb's Brigade holding off "Pickett's Charge" on July 3.

OPPOSITE: Waud's drawing of Gen. Winfield S. Hancock at Gettysburg. He played an important role at the battle, his troops on Cemetery Ridge bearing the brunt of Pickett's Charge.

HANCOCK AT GETTYSBURG —

ABOVE: The Gettysburg Address, as photographed by Brady and then presented in a lithograph produced by Sherwood Lithograph Co.

"Fourscore and seven years ago our fathers brought forth on this continent a new nation, conceived in liberty and dedicated to the proposition that all men are created equal.

Now we are engaged in a great civil war, testing whether that nation or any nation so conceived and so dedicated can long endure. We are met on a great battlefield of that war. We have come to dedicate a portion of it as a final resting place for those who died here that the nation might live. This we may, in all propriety, do. But in a larger sense, we cannot dedicate, we cannot consecrate, we cannot hallow this ground. The brave men, living and dead who struggled here have hallowed it far above our poor power to add or detract. The world will little note nor long remember what we say here, but it can never forget what they did here.

It is rather for us the living, we here be dedicated to the great task remaining before us—that from these honored dead we take increased devotion to that cause for which they here gave the last full measure of devotion—that we here highly resolve that these dead shall not have died in vain, that this nation shall have a new birth of freedom, and that government of the people, by the people, for the people shall not perish from the earth."

Lee was supposedly meant to be receiving intelligence from Maj. Gen. J. E. B. Stuart's cavalry, but Stuart had embarked on a raiding mission on the 26th and would be missing until July 2. Nevertheless, there were some vague reports of the Army of the Potomac's whereabouts. A Union cavalry brigade undertaking a reconnaissance was moving cautiously northward in Maryland and happened to bump into a Confederate infantry brigade just to the north of Gettysburg on the 30th. Both sides now tried to concentrate their forces there.

The battle proper opened on 1 July to the north of the town, with both sides feeding troops into the action as they arrived. Lee had wanted to make a powerful offensive push into the Union then secure good defensive ground for his entire force and wait for his opponents to attack. By the end of the first day, it was the Union troops who were holding good defensive ground to the south of Gettysburg. Lee knew that the onus would be on him to attack, but his army was still arriving.

On day two Lee decided that he would try to swing round the far left of the fish-hook-shaped Union line and also strike against its extreme right flank. The attack against the left began in the afternoon once the corps needed had arrived. The Union troops holding positions along the Emmitsburg Road were forced back to the summit of Cemetery Ridge, but the attackers were thwarted in turning the far left flank by the staunch defense of two high points, Little and Big Round Top. The move against the right made some progress, but the gains were abandoned when no reinforcements arrived.

For day three Lee, who was poorly, made a fateful decision to punch his way through the very center of the Union line—an uncharacteristically unimaginative strategy that some of his generals opposed—and some 12,000–15,000 troops were committed to what became known as "Pickett's Charge." Many Rebel troops failed to reach the Union positions on Cemetery Ridge, being cut down by intense rifle and cannon fire. Even fewer actually crossed the low stone wall that marked the front line. Within minutes the shattered Confederate units broke and fled, but no more than 5,000 returned to their own lines. The battle was effectively over—the "high tide of the Confederacy" had briefly arrived, but rapidly departed on Cemetery Ridge. It was only a matter of time now before the South was defeated.

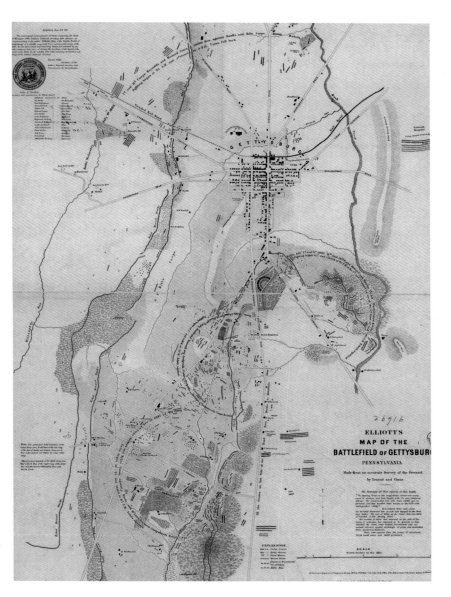

ABOVE: Elliott's map of the battlefield of Gettysburg "made from an accurate survey of the ground by transit and chain." It shows breastworks and rifle pits, graves of Union and Confederate soldiers, dead horses, roads and streets, relief by hachures, vegetation, drainage, houses, and the names of residents.

Date: July 10–September 7, 1863
Commanders: Union—Brig. Gen.
Quincy Gillmore; Confederate—Brig.
Gen. William Taliaferro
Troop strengths: Union—5,000;
Confederate—1,800
Casualties: Union—1,515 (246
killed, 880 wounded, and 389
missing); Confederate—174 (36
killed, 133 wounded, and 5 missing)

The Assault on Fort Wagner

Although not the most famous battle of the war, the assault on Fort Wagner by the 54th Massachusetts, an African-American regiment, served to show their critics that black soldiers were every bit as committed and every bit as brave as their white counterparts. It was recognized as such at the time, *The New York Tribune* commenting: "[the battle] made Fort Wagner such a name to the colored race as Bunker Hill had been for ninety years to the white Yankees."

Under the command of Brig. Gen. Quincy Gillmore, an ambitious leader who had shone at the siege of Fort Pulaski, the campaign against Charleston in 1863 started on Morris Island on July 10. The plan was to capture the island, place artillery on it, and bombard Fort Sumter into submission. With Sumter in Union hands, Charleston's fall would not be long in coming.

The surprise attack pushed the Confederate forces back, but Fort Wagner held out. The next day, the 11th, saw the Union forces repulsed. The scene was set for a more considered onslaught of the fort, on the 18th, after a suitably heavy bombardment.

RIGHT: Storming Fort Wagner, a Kurz & Allison lithograph showing William Carney on the ramparts.

ABOVE: Col. Robert G. Shaw (1837–63) commanded the 54th Massachusetts and died in the attack on the fort.

ABOVE LEFT: The Robert Gould Shaw and Massachusetts 54th Regiment Memorial is located across Beacon Street from the State House, Boston, MA.

Leading that assault up a narrow beach was Col. Robert G. Shaw and the 54th Massachusetts. They would lose their commanding officer and 42 percent of their men.

The fort was a very serious obstacle, protected by the ocean on the east and a swamp on the west, with a bombproof that could house over half of the garrison, parapets that rose thirty feet above the beach, a water-filled ditch, landmines, and other obstacles. It was stronger than the Confederates could have hoped, withstanding a day-long barrage by land batteries and the Union fleet. The weight of shot may have done superficial damage, but the Charleston Battalion who manned the ramparts suffered few casualties and were able to concentrate murderous fire on the attackers. The 54th's banner reached the parapet but their attack was thrown back at great cost to the unit. The follow-up troops—the 6th Connecticut and 48th New York—fared no better, particularly after the Confederates had managed to get three howitzers into position and rained canister fire upon the attackers. The Union gained a small foothold on the fort but Confederate counterattacks forced them to retreat.

The Confederate garrison held out for a further two months before slipping away at night.

Some 37 years after the battle, Sgt. William Carney, one-time slave, received the Medal of Honor for his bravery in the action, his citation reading, "When the color sergeant was shot down, this soldier grasped the flag, led the way to the parapet, and planted the colors thereon. When the troops fell back he brought off the flag, under a fierce fire in which he was twice severely wounded."

Date: September 19–20, 1863
Commanders: Union—Maj. Gen. William S. Rosecrans; Confederate—Gen. Braxton Bragg
Troop strengths: Union—62,000; Confederate—65,000
Casualties: Union—16,200 (1,656 killed, 9,756 wounded, and 4,757 missing); Confederate—18,500 (2,312 killed, 14,674 wounded, and 1,486 missing)

The Battle of Chickamauga

Aside from Grant's ongoing struggle to capture Vicksburg, there was little action elsewhere in the civil war's western theater during the first six months of 1863. Rosecrans' Army of the Cumberland remained at Murfreesboro, while Bragg remained stationed at Tullahoma. After his superiors demanded action, Rosecrans made a successful attempt to push Bragg all the way back to Chattanooga between June 23 and July 2. After another lengthy delay, the Army of the Cumberland moved on Chattanooga aided by the Army of the Ohio, which pushed towards Knoxville, TN, from its base at Lexington, KY.

RIGHT: Waud's sketch of the Confederate line advancing.

Bragg was forced to abandon Chattanooga on September 8 and withdrew to LaFayette in northwest Georgia. Coming on top of the defeat at Gettysburg on July 3 and the loss of Vicksburg on the next day, the news that Rosecrans was pushing into the heart of the Confederacy along various routes warranted immediate action. A corps from the Army of Northern Virginia was rushed to Bragg's aid and the latter decided to attack Rosecrans, who was still trying to concentrate his various corps outside Chattanooga. Partly due to the densely wooded terrain the two armies eventually stumbled into each other along Chickamauga Creek late on September 18.

The first day of the battle saw fierce if confused fighting in which neither side gained any clear advantages, but matters changed on the 20th. Rosecrans issued faulty orders that moved some divisions unnecessarily, thereby leaving a gap in his center through which poured the corps of troops from the Army of Northern Virginia. The Army of the Cumberland's center and right flank collapsed and many troops, roughly a third of the total and including Rosecrans, simply abandoned the field. Only the staunch resistance of the surviving left flank under Maj. Gen. George Thomas, soon to be dubbed the "Rock of Chickamauga," prevented total disaster.

The "River of Death," so called by Native Americans, had lived up to its name. Both sides had suffered around 28 percent losses in the two-day struggle around Chickamauga, the biggest battle in the western theater. Despite having the possible opportunity of destroying the greater part of Rosecrans' shattered command on the 20th, Bragg made little immediate effort to pursue. The Union forces fell back to Chattanooga, and Confederate forces placed the city under siege a few days after the battle. The Union forces would remain bottled up until relieved in late October. Rosecrans' career was ruined by that one mistake at Chickamauga; he was relieved of his command to be replaced by Thomas.

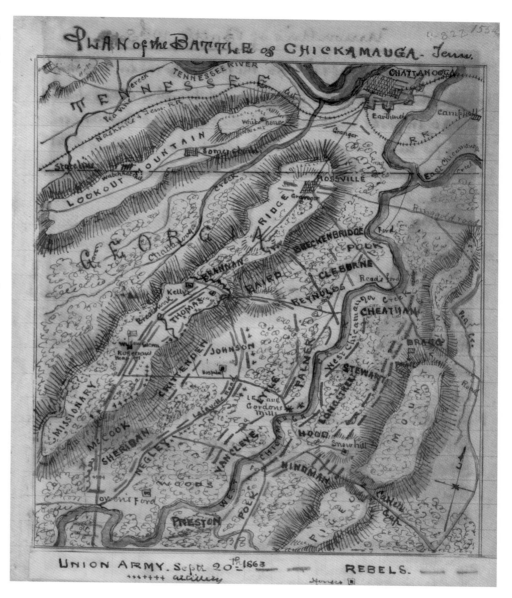

ABOVE: A Sneden map showing the location of forces on the second day of the battle, before the Confederates broke through the Union line and sent the majority heading back toward Chattanooga.

Date: November 24–25, 1863
Commanders: Union—Maj. Gen.
Ulysses S. Grant; Confederate—
Gen. Braxton Bragg
Troop strengths: Union—61,000;
Confederate—44,000
Casualties: Union—5,824 (753
killed, 4,722 wounded, and 349
missing); Confederate—6,667 (361
killed, 2,160 wounded, and 4,146
missing, mostly prisoners)

The Battle of Chattanooga

Following his defeat at the Battle of Chickamauga in September 1863, the commander of the Union Army of the Cumberland, Maj. Gen. William Rosecrans, withdrew into Chattanooga, where he was besieged by Bragg's Army of Tennessee. The situation was stalemated over the next several weeks, despite two corps of the Union's Army of the Potomac, under Maj. Gen. Joseph Hooker, being rushed some 1,200 miles to Bridgeport, just thirty miles from Rosecrans. Matters began to improve on October 17, when Grant was made commander of all the Union troops between the Mississippi River and Allegheny Mountains.

Grant moved on Chattanooga the same day, sacking Rosecrans as he went and appointing Maj. Gen. George Thomas in his stead. Ten days later, Union troops slipped into the city, partially lifting the siege. Grant was well aware that the Confederates still

OPPOSITE: Thure de Thulstrup's view of Chattanooga as published in *Prang's War Pictures* shows, "In the group of three figures in the left foreground will be recognized the compact form of General Grant lifting his field-glass to his eye; on his left stands General Granger; while the heroic proportions of General Thomas, then newly christened the 'Rock of Chicamauga,' stand out boldly against the horizon. Near this historic trio may be seen a signal officer vainly endeavoring to communicate with General Sherman, for whose relief the attack immediately in front has been made. Farther in rear stand officers of the staff in attendance upon the principal commanders. To the right is the corps headquarters flag and color-guard with their horses."

ABOVE: Portrait of Maj. Gen. George H. Thomas—"The Rock of Chickamauga." He was instrumental in Grant's victory at Chattanooga, and soundly beat Hood at the battle of Nashville.

ABOVE LEFT: Maj. Gen. George H. Thomas' charge near Orchard Knob on November 24 as created by Kurz & Allison. Gen. Thomas (1816–70) served with great distinction in the Union army despite being a Virginian. Evidently a difficult personality, he was nevertheless averse to self-promotion or what he considered unwarranted advancement, so his military achievements have been overshadowed by his more publicity-friendly contemporaries.

held two key positions outside the city—Lookout Mountain to the west and Missionary Ridge to the south and east—and therefore called on reinforcements in the guise of Brig. Gen. William Sherman's Army of the Tennessee, which was based around Memphis.

Bragg was so confident of the impregnability of his defenses that he actually sent some 20,000 men to besiege another Union army that had become stalled at Knoxville in northeast Tennessee due to supply problems. For his part, Grant felt ready to attack once Sherman's forces and the two corps of the Army of the Potomac had arrived. The first attack came on November 24, when he unleashed Hooker and Sherman against Lookout Mountain and Missionary Ridge, respectively. Sherman, whose troops had only just arrived in Chattanooga, was thrown back, but Hooker's men stormed the mountain against light opposition in what was dubbed "the battle above the clouds."

The first day of the battle had captured one of the key Confederate positions, and Grant resolved to fling all of his forces against Missionary Ridge on the second day. Sherman attacked on the Confederate right and Hooker moved against the left, but neither made any significant progress. The fighting turned thanks to Thomas's Army of the Cumberland. His troops faced three lines of entrenchments but took the first line without difficulty in what was meant to be no more than a supporting attack. Rather than pause, they continued the assault, taking the two remaining lines of Confederate defenses. When they reached the top of the ridge, the defenders broke and fled. Grant then sent Sherman to relieve Knoxville in a brief campaign that ended on December 6. Bragg was dismissed and, with Tennessee securely in Union hands, the stage was set for Sherman to launch his drive towards Atlanta, GA, the following spring.

Date: May 8–21, 1864
Commanders: Union—Lt. Gen. Ulysses S. Grant; Confederate—Gen. Robert E. Lee
Troop strengths: Union—100,000; Confederate—52,000
Casualties: Union—18,399 (2,725 killed, 13,416 wounded, 2,258 captured/missing); Confederate—12,687 (1,515 killed, 5,414 wounded, 5,758 captured/missing)

The Battle of Spotsylvania

The Union had ended 1863 in a dominant position after Grant's victory at Chattanooga. It was to be his last victory in the west. In March 1864 Lincoln promoted him lieutenant-general and gave him command of all Union armies. Their strategy in the east would be simple and bloody: an offensive that sought out Lee's Army of Northern Virginia, intending if necessary to use Union numbers to grind out attritional victory.

Three thrusts were planned under generals Butler (the Army of the James); Sigel (West Virginia); and Meade, with Grant in attendance. Butler ended bottled up by Gen. Beauregard and in a passive position after the Bermuda Hundred Campaign. Sigel started the (Shenandoah) Valley Campaigns, but when he was ignominiously defeated at New Market on May 15, 1864, Sigel was replaced by Hunter. He, in turn, would be forced to retreat by Jubal Early (see page 50).

Meade and Grant's Overland Campaign started at the battle of the Wilderness (May 5–6), where the Union Army of the Potomac sustained higher casualties than Lee's (17,666—2,246 killed, 12,037 wounded, 3,383 captured/missing—as against 11,033—1,477 killed, 7,866 wounded, 1,690 captured/missing) but were not deflected from their plan. Withdrawing after the battle, the Army of the Potomac was heartened to see that they were not, as had happened so many times before, retreating, but continuing on into Virginia. By the early hours of the 7th, the Union troops had left the Wilderness and reached open ground. Lee, who had been forced for medical reasons to replace two of his corps commanders—the badly wounded James Longstreet by Maj. Gen. Richard H. Anderson, and the ill Ambrose P. Hill by Maj. Gen. Jubal A. Early—sent their two corps in pursuit: J. E. B. Stuart's cavalry reaching the Spotsylvania Courthouse crossroads just in time to hold up the Union advance.

RIGHT: First of a series of 32 pen and ink maps drawn by Mr. Robert E.L. Russell showing the development of the Battle of Spotsylvania Courthouse, May 8-21, 1864. This shows the opening position on, May 8 at 09:00.

The battle lasted nearly two weeks. Both sides dug in, the Confederates' defensive line forming a salient nicknamed the "Mule Shoe." An attack on the Mule Shoe on May 10 by Col. Emory Upton took the position but insufficiently reinforced, was repulsed by a counterattack. On May 12 60,000 men attacked the salient again. Hancock's corps smashed through the defenses, but was driven out of the "Bloody Angle," after a day of hand-to-hand fighting as fierce as any of the war. Significant casualties—5,000 Confederates and 6,800 from the Union—and heavy rain limited Grant's attacking options for the next four days, before another major attack on the 18th convinced him that the position was too strong to attack further. After holding off a counterattack by Lt. Gen. Richard S. Ewell's corps on May 19, Grant ordered a move south to outflank Lee's army, and in the process forced Lee to do the same.

ABOVE: Another of L. Prang & Co. Civil War illustrations by Thure de Thulstrup shows Union troops launching a surprise attack on a salient that later became known as "Bloody Angle."

Date: May 7–September 2, 1864
Commanders: Union—Maj. Gen.
William T. Sherman; Confederate—
Gen. Joseph E. Johnston, replaced
by Lt. Gen. John Bell Hood
Troop strengths: Union—98,000
rising to over 110,000;
Confederate—50,000 rising to 65,000
Casualties: Union—31,687;
(4,423 killed, 22,822 wounded,
4,442 missing/captured);
Confederate—34,979; (3,044 killed,
18,952 wounded, 12,983 missing/
captured)

Sherman's Atlanta Campaign

Gen. William Tecumseh Sherman (1820–91) has been called the "first modern general" and had a stellar military career that culminated in his role as Commanding General of the Army (1869–83), after his close friend Grant became president. Sherman started at West Point as a sixteen-year-old cadet going on to join the artillery as a second lieutenant. He was commissioned as a colonel in the 13th U.S. Infantry Regiment at the start of the Civil War and fought at the first battle of Bull Run. Promoted soon after to brigadier-general, he was promoted again in 1862 after the battle of Shiloh where he was wounded twice and had three horses shot from under him. A remorseless enemy, he took over from Grant in the west, and planned a campaign that would lead to Atlanta, GA: the second most important city of the Confederacy. His command comprised three armies: Maj. Gen. George H. Thomas' Army of the Cumberland (60,000), Maj. Gen. James B. McPherson's Army of Tennessee (30,000), and Maj. Gen. John M. Schofield's Army of Ohio (17,000). Opposing him, the Confederate Gen. Joseph E. Johnston's Army of Tennessee had fewer men, but they were in a strong defensive position, occupying Rocky Face Ridge, commanding the surrounding mountainous terrain and deep river valleys between Sherman and Atlanta.

Sherman's first move was to try to fix Johnston at Rocky Face Ridge with the Army of the Cumberland while the Army of Tennessee moved to Resaca, where it would cut Johnston's supply lines and force the Confederates to pull back toward Atlanta. Unfortunately, when McPherson reached Resaca on May 9 he found a large Confederate garrison and was forced to withdraw, enabling Johnston's forces to pull back to Resaca on May 12, where he expected to be reinforced by Lt. Gen. Leonidas Polk's corps.

Sherman followed Johnston, attacking Resaca on May 13–15. When Johnston withdrew further south, Sherman moved to outflank the Confederate defenses, and

Johnston pulled back again toward Cassville. Sherman again moved to outflank Johnston, and the two sides met at Dallas, GA, on May 25, fighting a series of battles over four days at New Hope Church, Pumpkinvine Creek, and Pickett's Mills before Sherman again attempted to move round Johnston's left flank. He was blocked at Kennesaw Mountain, near Marietta, on June 27. Johnston and his army were well dug in protecting Marietta and the Western & Atlantic Railroad that supplied Atlanta

For the first time in the campaign, Sherman attempted a frontal assault rather than forcing the Confederates to withdraw by flanking maneuvers, thinking that losses at Kolb's Farm some days earlier had stretched Johnston. The plan backfired as his attacks were beaten back and he lost nearly 3,000 men, although Johnston then withdrew across the Chattahoochee River, and then into Atlanta's fortifications. On July 17 Jefferson Davis relieved Johnston of command, appointing Gen. John Bell Hood in his place. Hood (1831–79) had graduated from West Point and joined Gen. Robert E. Lee as a brigade commander at the start of the war. Wounded at Gettysburg and Chickamauga, where he lost his right leg, he was known for being rash but brave. He took over command of the Army of Tennessee in a difficult position, with three Union columns under Schofield, McPherson, and Thomas converging on Atlanta.

Hood took the opportunity to attack while Sherman's armies were separated, when Thomas' Army of the Cumberland crossed Peachtree Creek. On July 20, he attacked with two corps led by Lt. Gen. Alexander P. Stewart and Lt. Gen. William J. Hardee—a total of 20,000 men—and initially threatened the Union lines, but the Confederates were beaten back at dusk losing 5,000 men in the battle.

Next, Hood decided to attack McPherson's Army of Tennessee at Decatur. Hardee's corps was dispatched on July 21 to outflank McPherson and to attack him in the rear, while the remainder of Hood's forces pulled back into prepared fortifications north of Atlanta. Hardee attacked early on July 22, but as at Peachtree Creek, the Union troops were in well-prepared positions and the Confederates failed to break through, losing 7,500 men against the Union's 3,700. One of the killed, however, was Gen. McPherson, shot dead after refusing to surrender when he blundered into the Confederate lines.

Sherman planned to attack Atlanta from the west. Hood's army was still mobile, and he tried to counter Sherman's plans but suffered heavy losses at the battle of Ezra Church on July 28, and he was forced to abandon his offensive strategy and withdraw into Atlanta. But as Sherman tightened his grip on the city in the following weeks, Hood sent two corps south towards Jonesboro in a final attempt to avoid being encircled and cut off, but the Union forces were well entrenched and easily repulsed the Confederates' attack on August 31. With Lt. Gen. W. J. Hardee's corps isolated at Jonesboro and Stephen D. Lee's pinned down outside Atlanta, Hood had no option but to abandon the city if he was to save the remnants of his army. He loaded as many supplies as he could onto railway carriages before destroying the remainder, and evacuated the city on September 1.

The next day, September 2, the Sherman entered Atlanta, sending a cable—"Atlanta is ours, and fairly won"—announcing his triumph.

ABOVE: Alfred Waud's sketch of Gen. John Bell Hood (1831–79). Confederate commander Hood acquired the reputation for being a rash but brave commander. After West Point he worked as a junior officer in California and Texas before joining Gen. Robert E. Lee as a brigade commander at the start of the war. He lost the use of his left arm at the battle of Gettysburg and then was wounded again at Chickamauga where he lost his right leg. Age 33 he was made temporary commander of the Army of Tennessee but proved inadequate and was relieved of command after defeat at Nashville. After the war he worked as a cotton broker and died of yellow fever in New Orleans in 1879.

OPPOSITE: Sherman and his generals in the Atlanta and Georgia campaigns, as pictured by Currier & Ives. L–R: James B. McPherson, Henry W. Slocum, Francis P. Blair Jr., George H. Thomas, Alpheus S. Williams, Oliver O. Howard, Sherman, John W. Geary, John M. Schofield, Jefferson C. Davis, William B. Hazen, H. Judson Kilpatrick, and John A. Logan.

Date: May 31–June 12, 1864
Commanders: Union—Lt. Gen.
Ulysses S. Grant; Confederate—Gen.
Robert E. Lee
Troop strengths: Union—110,000;
Confederate—60,000
Casualties: Union—12,737
(1,844 killed, 9,077 wounded,
1,816 captured/missing);
Confederate—5,287 (788 killed,
3,376 wounded, 1,123 captured/
missing)

The Battle of Cold Harbor

After Spotsylvania, Grant moved south hoping to cut Lee off from Richmond, and destroy the Confederates in open battle, where the Army of the Potomac's advantage in numbers (110,000 compared to 60,000) would show to the greatest effect. This was the last thing that Lee wanted, but during his withdrawal from Spotsylvania the Union forces had an opportunity to engage him as his troops marched south, but Maj. Gen. Gouverneur K. Warren's V Corps missed Lee's army as it marched past and Lee gained the sanctuary of the North Anna, where the next battle took place.

On May 23, as the main bulk of Union forces crossed, thinking Lee was retreating, they came onto a cleverly prepared inverted V defensive position. Lee, at the critical juncture of the battle fell ill and to this day there is debate as to whether the Confederates lost an opportunity to inflict a strong reverse on the Union army. Instead, Grant was able to slip away and Lee was forced back towards Richmond.

They met again at the Old Cold Harbor road junction. First, Maj. Gen. Philip H. Sheridan's cavalry drove back the Confederate cavalry under Lee's nephew Maj. Gen. Fitzhugh Lee on May 31, but the Confederate infantry held firm and Sheridan withdrew. Both sides tried to seize control of the crossroads and by June 2 had dug in over a seven-mile long front. Grant, concerned about the swampy ground of the Chickahominy River on his left flank, decided to stop his outflanking maneuver and attack head on.

RIGHT: A Timothy O'Sullivan photograph showing Federal troops occupying a line of breastworks on the north bank of the North Anna River.

ABOVE: Kurz & Allison lithograph of the battle of Cold Harbor.

It was a bad mistake, and one he would always rue, saying in his memoirs, "I have always regretted that last assault at Cold Harbor." The Union suffered severe casualties and when Grant realized he was unable to break through Lee's army, he was forced to continue his flanking attacks, this time moving south of Richmond towards Petersburg.

Estimates for the casualties at Cold Harbor vary—particularly for the day of the main assault, when Lee's careful defensive positions with their interlocked fields of fire and artillery positions wreaked havoc—but while the Northern press fulminated against the "butcher's bill," and the South hoped that this might cause Lincoln to lose the 1864 presidential election, Grant moved quickly to improve his position, disengaging, crossing the James, and threatening Petersburg. Whatever the cost, after Cold Harbor Lee was forced onto the back foot and spent most of the rest of the war defending Richmond and Petersburg.

Battle of Cedar Creek
Date: October 19, 1864
Commanders: Union—Gen. Philip Sheridan; Confederate—Gen. Jubal Early
Troop strengths: Union—31,610; Confederate—21,102
Casualties: Union—5,665 (644 killed, 3,430 wounded, 1,591 missing); Confederate—2,910 (320 killed, 1,540 wounded, 1,050 missing)

BELOW: Another sketch by Waud: Early's army falling back upon Winchester.

Campaigns in the Shenandoah Valley

In March 1864, after Grant took over command of all the Union armies, he planned three major attacks on the Confederates—the Overland Campaign by the Army of the Potomac directed at Lee; the Army of the James was to attack in Virginia; and in the Shenandoah Valley, Franz Sigel opened the Valley Campaigns. His defeat at New Market led to his replacement by Maj. Gen. David Hunter.

Lee sent Lt. Gen. Jubal Early to attack Hunter in the Shenandoah Valley with the dual intentions of curtailing Hunter's progress into Virginia so forcing Grant to send him reinforcements and thus reducing the Army of the Potomac's significantly superior manpower over the Army of Northern Virginia.

Early quickly moved into Maryland toward Washington. Grant was forced to send reinforcements (primarily VI Corps under Maj. Gen. (of Volunteers) Horatio G. Wright) and Early was held up long enough at the Monocacy on July 9 to allow time for reinforcing the defenses of Washington. Early arrived at Fort Stevens to the northwest of Washington on July 11, attacked without success and withdrew, pursued by Union forces. By July 20 Wright thought that the threat had dissipated and withdrew, but Early attacked at Kernstown on July 24, defeating Brig. Gen. George Crook, and continued his advance to attack the railroad in Maryland and burn Chambersburg, PA.

LEFT: Kurz & Allison's lithograph of the battle of Winchester, showing Sheridan's attack.

This was too much for Grant, who sent his cavalry general, Philip Sheridan, to take over. Sheridan (1831–88) had been on Maj. Gen. Halleck's staff before performing brilliantly as a cavalry commander first at Booneville, MS, and then as a corps commander at Perryville, Stones River, Chickamauga, and Chattanooga. Grant brought him to the east to command the cavalry of the Army of the Potomac on April 5, 1864. On August 7, he took over command of the Army of the Shenandoah and, after a number of minor engagements, defeated Early in the bloody third battle at Winchester on September 19. Further engagements culminated in the battle that effectively ended the campaign and materially assisted in the re-election of Lincoln: the battle of Cedar Creek on October 19.

BELOW: "Sheridan's Ride" from Winchester as depicted for Prang's *War Pictures* by Thule de Thulstrup.

Early attacked the Army of the Shenandoah while Sheridan was ten miles away returning from a conference in Washington. Wright was in charge but it was Crook's Army of West Virginia that was taken by surprise in an early morning attack under the cover of fog. Desperate defense allowed Wright to reorganize but it took Sheridan's arrival on the battlefield, after a famous ride from Winchester, to settle matters. As the victorious Confederates pillaged the Union supplies, Sheridan reformed his men and with cavalry under Custer and Merritt on the wings, attacked at around 16:00. The Union attack quickly reversed the position, forcing Early's army to retreat and give up its gains.

That was the end of the campaign. Sheridan was promoted major-general and returned to the Army of the Potomac where he continued to perform with élan. Early, when he finally returned to Gen. Robert E. Lee, was told to go home, his military career over.

Date: June 19, 1864
Commanders: Union—Capt. John Winslow; Confederate—Capt. Raphael Semmes
Naval strengths: Union—USS *Kearsarge*; Confederate—CSS *Alabama*
Casualties: Union—1 killed, 2 wounded; Confederate—ship sunk: 40 dead, 70 captured

Kearsarge defeats *Alabama*

Raphael Semmes (1809–77) served in the U.S. Navy 1826–60 but joined the Confederate States Navy when war began. Captain of the commerce raider CSS *Alabama* from August 1862 until she sank in June 1864, during this period he took 69 prizes. Escaping on the British yacht *Deerhound* after the engagement with *Kearsarge*, in 1865 he was promoted rear admiral and commanded the James River Squadron. After the destruction of the Confederate navy he was appointed brigadier-general in the Confederate army and his sailors became infantrymen, the "Naval Brigade."

The battle between *Kearsarge* and *Alabama* started when *Alabama* put into Cherbourg on June 11, in need of a refit after two years' raiding northern commercial shipping. Word got out quickly and the sloop of war USS *Kearsarge* arrived on the 14th.

RIGHT: "Hauling Down the Flag." J.O. Davidson's view of the *Kearsarge* fighting *Alabama* as produced for L. Prang & Co.'s *War Pictures*. Note on the *Kearsarge*'s deck the 11-inch pivot gun, which did so much damage to the enemy.

Its master, Captain John Winslow, had served in the U.S. Navy since 1827 and he and Semmes had served together on the *Cumberland*, a sailing frigate that was later sunk at Hampton Roads by *Virginia*.

Winslow had taken command of the *Kearsarge* in 1863 and spent his first fruitless months searching for Confederate raiders. During this time, however, he drilled his gun crews assiduously. *Kearsarge* was off Flushing when Winslow heard that *Alabama* had put into Cherbourg, and immediately set sail for France.

Semmes challenged *Kearsarge* and steamed out of harbor escorted by the French ironclad *Couronne*, there to ensure the combat remained in international waters. At 10:50 Winslow headed for *Alabama*, which opened fire at a range of about a mile. Winslow later wrote, "The position of the vessels was now broadside and broadside, but it was soon apparent that Captain Semmes did not seek close action. I became then fearful, lest after some fighting he would again make for the shore. To defeat this, I determined to keep full speed on, and with a port helm to run under the stern of the *Alabama* and rake, if he did not prevent it by sheering and keeping his broadside to us ... As a consequence the *Alabama* was forced with a full head of steam into a circular track during the engagement. The effect of this maneuver was such that at the last of the action, when the *Alabama* would have made off, she was near 5 miles from the shore, and had the action continued from the first in parallel lines, with her head inshore, the line of jurisdiction would no doubt have been reached. The firing of the *Alabama* from the first was rapid and wild. Toward the close of the action her firing became better. Our men, who had been cautioned against rapid firing without direct aim, were much more deliberate, and the instructions given to point the heavy guns below rather than above the water line and clear the deck with the lighter ones was fully observed. ... The effect of the training of our men was evident. Nearly every shot from our guns was telling fearfully on the *Alabama*, and on the seventh rotation on the circular track she winded, setting fore-trysail and two jibs, with head inshore. Her speed was now retarded, and, by winding, her port broadside was presented to us, with only two guns bearing ... I saw now that she was at our mercy, and a few more guns, well directed, brought down her flag. ... Shortly after this her boats were seen to be lowering, and an officer in one of them came alongside and informed us that the ship had surrendered and was fast sinking. In twenty minutes from this time the *Alabama* went down."

As *Alabama* sank, most of her crew were picked up by *Kearsarge* but the British yacht *Deerhound* saved Semmes and most of his officers, who thereby escaped capture and imprisonment, to the anger of the crew of the *Kearsarge*.

ABOVE: Photograph of USS *Kearsarge*'s 11-inch Dahlgren smoothbore cannon.

Date: September 18–December 27, 1864

Commanders: Union—Maj. Gen. John Schofield and Maj. Gen. George H. Thomas; Confederate— Lt. Gen. John Bell Hood

Troop strengths: Union—34,000 (Schofield) and 26,000 (Thomas); Confederate—39,000

Casualties: Union—over 5,000; Confederate—over 10,000 including desertions

Franklin-Nashville Campaign

Hood's Tennessee Campaign saw the second largest of the Confederate armies defeated and practically destroyed in three short months.

After the fall of Atlanta, Hood moved north, threatening Sherman's lines of communication, which stretched to Chattanooga. Initially Sherman pursued Hood, but with Grant's approval for his planned move toward Savannah, he left Maj. Gen. George H. Thomas' Army of the Cumberland to deal with the Confederates while he prepared to live off the land on his March to the Sea.

He could not have left the theater in better hands. Thomas—the "Rock of Chickamauga"—was one of the most successful generals of the war and had proved his worth on countless occasions. He was no self-publicist and did not get on well with Grant, who dubbed him "slow," but postwar Sherman said of him, "During the whole war his services were transcendent."

RIGHT: Kurz & Allison lithograph showing the battle of Franklin.

Hood waited in Florence to join forces with his cavalry under Maj. Gen. Nathan Bedford Forrest who had raided Union supply lines in Tennessee doing great damage at Johnsonville, an important logistical node on the Tennessee River. On November 16, Hood received word that Sherman was leaving Atlanta. Rather than following him into Georgia as Thomas and Sherman expected, he moved north from Florence on November 21, heading toward Franklin and Nashville, planning to get between the two Union forces—Thomas in Nashville and Schofield in Pulaski, TN. Schofield, meanwhile, moved his two infantry corps and dug in around Columbia, blocking Hood, who then outflanked Schofield and struck north to Spring Hill. Schofield, realizing that the Confederates had passed him, had to move back toward Franklin. On November 29 Hood had a great opportunity to do exactly what he had planned: confront the smaller Union force before it could link up with Thomas, but miscommunication and bad management allowed Schofield to slip past the Confederate army and reach Franklin on the 30th.

ABOVE: Photograph by George Barnard of the outer trenches on the last day of the battle in front of Nashville, showing the ground where the most desperate charges were made.

BELOW: Maj. Gen. John M. Schofield.

Hood's forces arrived in front of Franklin that afternoon and were immediately ordered to attack. One of the bloodiest engagements of the Civil War now took place, a stinging reverse to the Army of Tennessee who fought with unstinting bravery against a well-equipped and well-dug-in foe. They suffered 6,252 casualties, including 1,750 killed and 3,800 wounded. Among these were fourteen Confederate generals (six killed or mortally wounded, including Maj. Gen. Patrick Cleburne, seven wounded, and one captured) and 55 regimental commanders were casualties. Union losses, in spite of the heavy fighting which saw the Confederates break through in the center until repulsed by the reserve brigade under Emerson Opdycke, were reported as 189 killed, 1,033 wounded, and 1,104 missing.

Schofield withdrew after the battle, leaving Hood in control of Franklin. Hood asked for reinforcements, but there were none to be had, so the 26,500 men left to the army advanced on Nashville where the Union forces totaled around 55,000 men. Reaching the city on December 2, Hood dug in and waited for Thomas to attack, hoping to be able to hold the Union forces and counterattack. Thomas prepared carefully for the forthcoming battle—much to the irritation of Lincoln and Grant who thought he procrastinated—and it was not until December 15 that he attacked, with a diversionary assault on the Confederate right and wheeling attack on the left that would outflank them. The diversionary plan did not work, but on the Confederate left the Union cavalry took the redoubts that anchored their line, forcing the Confederate forces to retreat. The next day, December 16, saw them routed after a day's fighting, the attack by Brig. Gen. John McArthur's division finally leading to a headlong retreat towards Franklin. Union casualties in the battle were 387 killed, 2,562 wounded, and 112 missing. When the remnants of the Army of Tennessee finally reached Tupelo, MS, Hood resigned his command on January 13, 1865.

Date: June 9, 1864–April 3, 1865
Commanders: Union—Lt. Gen.
Ulysses S. Grant; Confederate—
Gen. Robert E. Lee
Troop strengths: Union—125,000 by
March 1865; Confederate—50,000
Casualties: Union—c. 42,000;
Confederate—c.28,000

The Siege of Petersburg and Richmond

After the costly debacle at Cold Harbor, Grant crossed the River James and headed toward Petersburg, the South's supply center, and a series of battles that would, eventually, lead to the surrender of the city, the nearby Confederate capital Richmond, and soon after the Army of Northern Virginia and with it the hopes of the Confederate states.

Much of the nine-month siege saw extensive trench warfare—it is often described as the forerunner of the battles of World War I—as Grant pursued a strategy of envelopment, attacking and cutting the rail links to the city, forcing Lee into a number of attritional battles that made use of the Union's superior manpower. As the final rail links were cut, to keep mobile Lee was forced to leave the area or undergo a real siege inside the Petersburg–Richmond lines.

The first assault on the lines around Petersburg took place on June 9; the second on June 15–18. Had either of these attacks been vigorously pursued it's possible that a breakthrough could have been effected early in the campaign. As it was, Gen. Beauregard

RIGHT: Kurz & Allison's print of the Fall of Petersburg.

was able to defend against the attacks until Lee sent him reinforcements—amounting to some 20,000 men. The Union troops, too, had been reinforced and had now swelled to 67,000. Their attack on the 18th made initial headway but foundered on Beauregard's new defensive line. Later that day Lee himself took over control of the battlefield and the day ended with over 11,000 Union casualties including nearly 2,000 dead.

For the next eight months the Union forces probed away, slowly encircling Petersburg's south and southwest; fighting northeast of the city toward Richmond, all the while reducing Lee's troop levels. There were nine major offensives, the third of which (July 26–30) saw battles in the crater created by the explosion of a huge mine under Confederate lines on July 30. It killed nearly 300 Confederates but the subsequently mishandled assault led to nearly 4,000 Union casualties including 500 dead.

With Early's defeat by Sheridan in the Shenandoah Valley and Sherman's men fighting their way north through the Carolinas, it became clear that the Union force levels were going to get much higher and so Lee decided he had to break out. He tried to do so at Fort Stedman on March 25, 1865, but was thrown back with serious losses (4,000 casualties compared to the Union's 1,000). A few days later, at Five Forks, Sheridan hammered another nail into the coffin, defeating Pickett and threatening Lee's South Side Railroad escape route. Lee realized the game was up, told Jefferson Davis that Petersburg and Richmond should be evacuated: there was no time to do so. On April 2 Grant ordered a general assault. Lee and what men he had escaped to the west as the city fell to the Union.

Date: August 5, 1864
Commanders: Union—Adm. David Farragut; Confederate—Cdre. Franklin Buchanan
Naval strengths: Union—4 ironclads and 14 other warships with 3,000 men; Confederate—1 ironclad and 3 gunboats with 417 men
Casualties: Union—145 killed and 177 wounded; Confederate—12 killed, 20 wounded, and 123 captured

The Battle of Mobile Bay

Louisiana's New Orleans, the South's most important port through which much of the supplies needed to fuel its military effort in the Civil War flowed, was captured by Union forces in 1862 and thereafter Mobile, AL, took its place. It was not for two years that Union naval forces turned their attention to the port, but in early August 1864 Farragut, the conqueror of New Orleans, sailed into Mobile Bay at the head of a large flotilla, one that included four relatively invulnerable turreted ironclads of the famed Monitor class and fourteen more vulnerable traditional wooden warships that had been lashed together in pairs.

The smaller Confederate flotilla commanded by Buchanan was considerably less impressive, with just three wooden gunboats, *Gaines*, *Morgan*, and *Selma*, and a single ironclad, the slow-moving *Tennessee*, which was modeled on the equally renowned *Merrimac*. The action began at around 05:30. Farragut, on board his flagship *Hartford*, led his command into the bay but his track took him under the guns of the bay's two main forts, Gaines on the eastern tip of Dauphin Island, and Morgan at the western end of Mobile Point. The entrance is just three miles wide and the forts' fire was accurate and devastating, especially that from Morgan since it was nearest to the Union flotilla.

Union casualties were severe, but much worse was soon to follow. The lead monitor, *Tecumseh*, hit a "torpedo" (actually a floating mine) as it made to attack *Tennessee* and rapidly sank. Farragut, impatient to close with the Confederate flotilla, famously ordered: "Damn the torpedoes. Full speed ahead." Buchanan moved out to attack at around 08:00 and Farragut responded by opening fire on *Tennessee*, his most dangerous opponent, as well instructing his own *Hartford* and other warships to ram the ironclad at regular intervals.

The *Tennessee* took this punishment for around sixty minutes but was itself unable to reply—it was too slow to ram the faster-moving Union warships and could not fire back because of defective fuses. The battering continued until the Southern ironclad was unable to maneuver and, with Buchanan out of action due to a broken leg, the fighting ended with his surrender at 10:00. Two of the gunboats were also captured. Farragut's clear-cut victory meant that the South's only really large port, and the center for blockade-running in the Gulf of Mexico, was sealed, although Mobile itself did not surrender until the last days of the war in April 1865.

OPPOSITE: Portrait of Cdre. Franklin Buchanan, C.S.N. (1800–74). A serving officer in the U.S. Navy for 45 years, Buchanan joined the Confederate side in 1861. His first command was the ironclad CSS *Virginia* but he had to relinquish command after he was wounded in the thigh at the battle of Hampton Roads. In 1862 he became admiral and commanded Confederate forces at Mobile Bay. He was wounded in the battle there, taken prisoner, and held for a year.

ABOVE: J. O. Davidson's rendition of the battle of Mobile Bay appeared in *Prang's War Pictures*. It shows the monitor *Tecumseh* capsizing after hitting a mine (called torpedoes in the Civil War).

Date: November 15–December 21, 1864
Commanders: Union—Maj. Gen. William T. Sherman; Confederate—Lt. Gen. William J. Hardee
Troop strengths: Union—62,000 men; Confederate—13,000
Casualties: Union—1,200; Confederate— over 1,600

Sherman's March to the Sea

Sherman, having taken Atlanta, proposed to head southeast toward Savannah, on the Georgia coast, before heading northward through the Carolinas. Hood proposed to live off the land on what today looks more akin to a medieval chevauchée than a modern campaign.

His plan approved, Sherman left Hood to Maj. Gen. John Schofield and Maj. Gen. George H. Thomas and prepared his men. He had 62,000 of them in two wings commanded by Maj. Gen. Henry W. Slocum and Maj. Gen. Oliver O. Howard.

Slocum (1827–94) had resigned his commission in 1856 to become a lawyer in 1858, but as a colonel and artillery instructor for the New York militia he was ready at the outbreak of war to become colonel of the 27th New York Infantry that he led at the First Bull Run. Howard (1830–1909)—known as the "Christian General"—had lost an arm but won a Congressional Medal of Honor at the battle of Fair Oaks in 1862.

Hood moved out on November 15 leaving the city of Atlanta in flames. Ahead of him was enemy territory, but it was lightly defended by local militia who were blown away by the seasoned Union troops. On November 22 at Macon the Georgia militia attacked a Union infantry rearguard detachment and suffered 500 casualties to the Union's 62.

Sherman cut a swathe through Georgia, destroying any infrastructure (such as railways) and foraging on the countryside, leaving scorched earth behind. William the Conqueror had harried the north of England in 1069–70 and it took years to recover: Sherman did the same to Georgia inside a month.

By December 10 Sherman's two wings were converging on the outskirts of Savannah, on the coast. There the Confederates had gathered a force of 15,000 men under Lt. Gen. William J. Hardee to defend the city. "Old Reliable" (1815–73) had graduated West

ABOVE: Waud shows Gen. Sherman reviewing his army in Savannah before starting on his new campaign. Noted on the reverse of the sketch: Among the mounted officers behind major General Sherman are Gen Williams, Logan, Slocum, Geary, Baird, Woods, Smith, & co.

Point in 1838, serving with the 2nd U.S. Dragoons in the Seminole Wars. He returned to teach at West Point 1853–60 and in 1855 published Hardee's Tactics (or properly *Rifle and Light Infantry Tactics for the Exercise and Manoeuvres of Troops When Acting as Light Infantry or Riflemen*) which was used extensively by both sides in the Civil War.

The Confederates hoped that the city's formidable defenses and port open to supplies from elsewhere in the Confederacy would enable Hardee to hold Savannah. Sherman's first move was to detach a division on December 13 to take Fort McAllister, 15 miles south of Savannah. U.S. Navy warships could now resupply his forces unmolested. Hardee, realizing he was about to be encircled and that the city would not be able to withstand a siege, decided to evacuate. His men escaped across the Savannah River on the night of December 20, and Sherman entered the city the next day, wiring President Lincoln to present the city "as a Christmas gift."

TOP: Before they left Atlanta, the Union troops burned any war resources, in particular those to do with the railroad, but left churches and hospitals intact.

ABOVE: XIV and XX Corps move out of Atlanta, November 15, 1864.

Date: April 2–9, 1865
Commanders: Union—Lt. Gen. Ulysses S. Grant; Confederate—Gen. Robert E. Lee
Troop strengths: Union—100,000 men; Confederate—28,000
Casualties: Union—9,700; Confederate—6,266 killed or wounded, 27,805 captured and paroled

The Army of Virginia Surrenders

When it became clear that Petersburg would fall, on the night of April 2–3 Lee headed west in the hope that he could join up with Joseph Johnston's army in North Carolina. He lost what advantage in time he had on the chasing Union army at Amelia Springs where he had hoped to pick up provisions. Unfortunately the final trains from Richmond had not made it. He was promised rations at Farmville, 25 miles west of Amelia Springs but by now the Union cavalry had caught up and his troops were involved in running battles. At Sayler's Creek he lost a quarter of his troops, some 8,000 men, to Sheridan.

Lee made one last attempt to break away, standing at the battle of Appomattox Courthouse, but surrounded by the enemy he surrendered at 15:00 along with some 2,349 infantry, 1,559 cavalry, and 2,576 artillery troops.

The terms agreed by Grant were generous and he showed great compassion toward the beaten Confederates, sending rations to Lee's soldiers. The Confederates officially surrendered their arms on April 12, 1865, bringing the war in Virginia to a close. In Washington, news of the surrender was marked by a 500-gun salute (for the earlier capture of Richmond, a 900-gun salute had been fired).

RIGHT: Kurz & Allison's lithograph showing the capitulation and surrender of Robert E. Lee and his army to Grant at Appomattox.

ABOVE: Timothy O'Sullivan's photograph of Appomattox Court House.

LEFT: Waud's sketch of Robert E. Lee leaving the McLean House following his surrender to Ulysses S. Grant.

With the surrender of the Army of Northern Virginia, Confederate defeat was inevitable. Jefferson F. Davis met with his cabinet and his senior officers, Generals Joseph Johnston and Pierre G. T. Beauregard, at Greensborough, NC, to discuss the situation. Davis wanted to continue the fight, but the generals and the majority of his cabinet wanted to sue for peace and on April 12, Davis conceded that Johnston should meet Sherman to discuss surrender terms. In fact he surrendered his army to Grant in the Carolinas on April 26.

The final military actions of the Civil War took place far from the main theaters of war: small-scale engagements occurred in the North Pacific between pro-Union and pro-Confederate fishing boats until news of the final surrender of the South reached them.